Romeo and Juliet
WILLIAM SHAKESPEARE

● for Key Stage 3 ●

Guide written by

Ron Simpson

D0529211

A *Letts* EXPLORE

First published 1998

Letts Educational
Aldine House
Aldine Place
London W12 8AW
0181 740 2266

Text © Ron Simpson

Sample questions Jeff Morton

Series editor Jo Kemp

Typeset by Jordan Publishing Design

Text design Jordan Publishing Design

Cover and text illustrations Ivan Allen

Design © BPP (Letts Educational) Ltd

Acknowledgements

British Library Cataloguing in Publication Data
A CIP record for this book is available from the British Library

ISBN 1 85758 923 8

Printed and bound in Great Britain

Ashford Colour Press, Gosport, Hampshire

Letts Educational is the trading name of BPP (Letts Educational) Ltd

■ Contents

ROMEO AND JULIET.

Panel 1

MONTAGUES AND CAPULETS... DEADLY ENEMIES!

I HATE HELL, ALL MONTAGUES AND THEE.

Panel 2

ROMEO AND HIS FRIENDS GATE-CRASH THE CAPULETS' PARTY.

O THEN I SEE QUEEN MAB HAS BEEN WITH YOU.

MY MIND MISGIVES SOME CONSEQUENCE.

Panel 3

LOVE AT FIRST SIGHT.

GIVE ME MY SIN AGAIN.

YOU KISS BY TH' BOOK.

Panel 4

MY ONLY LOVE SPRUNG FROM MY ONLY HATE.

ROMEO ESCAPES FROM HIS FRIENDS.

IT IS THE EAST AND JULIET IS THE SUN.

PARTING IS SUCH SWEET SORROW THAT I SHALL SAY GOOD NIGHT TILL IT BE MORROW.

⑤

ROMEO AND JULIET MARRY IN SECRET, IN SPITE OF FRIAR LAWRENCE'S DOUBTS.

THESE VIOLENT DELIGHTS HAVE VIOLENT ENDS.

⑥

TYBALT STABS MERCUTIO.

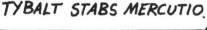

ROMEO STABS TYBALT...

⑦

AND IS BANISHED. JULIET'S FATHER HAS PLANS.

⑧

O'THURSDAY... SHE SHALL BE MARRIED TO THIS NOBLE EARL.

THE WEDDING NIGHT.

IT WAS THE LARK, THE HERALD OF THE MORN, NO NIGHTINGALE.

9

JULIET REFUSES TO OBEY HER FATHER.

AND YOU BE MINE, I'LL GIVE YOU TO MY FRIEND.

10

THE FRIAR HAS A SOLUTION.

IF THOU DAREST, I'LL GIVE THEE REMEDY.

NO WARMTH, NO BREATH SHALL TESTIFY THOU LIVEST...

11

THIS DISTILLING LIQUOR DRINK THOU OFF.

IN THE MORNING... THERE ART THOU DEAD.

12

ROMEO IS SUMMONED BACK TO VERONA...

HER BODY SLEEPS IN CAPELS' MONUMENT.

BUT THE OTHER MESSENGER NEVER ARRIVED.

I COULD NOT SEND IT, HERE IT IS AGAIN.

THREE DEATHS IN JULIET'S TOMB.

THIS IS THY SHEATH; THERE REST AND LET ME DIE.

THE FEUD ENDS.

A GLOOMING PEACE THIS MORNING WITH IT BRINGS.

■ Who's Who in *Romeo and Juliet*

Romeo

Romeo's character in the play is simply that of the young lover: Benvolio and Mercutio may hint at a time when he behaved differently, but we never see it. The variety of the character comes in the contrast between his two loves and in the various situations in which he is placed. In love with Rosaline, he is conventionally lovesick and melancholy, but the sight of Juliet transforms his life. The formality of their first vows immediately suggests a more mature emotion. Thereafter, Romeo's only preoccupation is Juliet and his love for her. From this come such changes as his new-found tolerance of Capulets, and all his impetuous decisions from marriage to suicide. Within his one fixed idea (marriage to Juliet), Romeo reacts to circumstance. He responds to plans drawn up by Friar Lawrence, Juliet and the Nurse and his moods switch from delight to despair: in Act 3, Scene 3, for instance, he moves from attempted suicide to 'a joy past joy'.

Juliet

At nearly 14, Juliet displays remarkable maturity. Like Romeo, once they have met, there is only one point of focus for her life. However, her character is presented in a rather different way from Romeo's. For instance, we see her home life, whereas Romeo's parents, though appearing in the play, do not take part in intimate scenes with him. Juliet at home is obedient to her parents, until her love for Romeo makes obedience impossible. She is spirited, intelligent and independent, but not a rebel for the sake of it and, despite her boldness in the secret marriage, she is concerned with doing what is right. Perhaps rather sadly, her most natural and affectionate scenes are with her Nurse rather than her parents, though all three will ultimately let her down. Juliet becomes passionate and single-minded, capable of the most intense rapture (as in the opening to Act 3, Scene 2) and unblinking courage in her assumed death (probably more even than in her suicide).

Tybalt

Tybalt is a unique character in *Romeo and Juliet*. The feud between Capulets and Montagues is, we presume, going on all the time: servants of both families brawl in the streets, the heads of the families are drawn in and threaten each other. However, Tybalt is the only named family member (except, in some editions, the silent Petruchio who accompanies him) to go out looking for trouble. We see him in Act 1, Scene 5, furious and insulted at Romeo's appearance at the feast, and his pursuit of Romeo brings his own death and a change of tone and direction in the play. In Tybalt we see the violent hatred of the feud still alive. What he is like in other respects we do not know, but Juliet calls him 'my dearest cousin'.

Mercutio

Mercutio is the character who has most individuality away from the Romeo-and-Juliet love story, though his two accidental contributions to that story are very important. Firstly, he and Benvolio take the unwilling Romeo to the Capulets' feast and, secondly, his death at the hands of Tybalt causes Romeo's killing of Tybalt and banishment from Verona. Mercutio's character belongs to the comparatively light-hearted first half of the play and his death begins the darkening of mood. He is witty and cynical, the opposite of the romantic figure that Romeo becomes, and his exchanges with Romeo and Benvolio are enjoyable examples of youthful word-play and amiably imaginative insults. We must be careful, however, not to admire Mercutio too much. His scene with the Nurse is a series of obscene jokes and is typical of his love of mockery. He seems unlikely actually to achieve anything; he does, in fact, achieve a brave death.

The Nurse

There are two main elements to the Nurse's role in the play. Like Mercutio, she contributes much to the humour of the first half and, like Friar Lawrence, she is an essential part of the secret plot: as go-between. In her first scene with Lady Capulet and Juliet (Act 1, Scene 3) she launches into a very long speech which is barely relevant and full of digressions. This establishes her character. Her affection for Juliet and desire to help her are obvious, but her appearances are mainly enjoyed for her gossip, her inability to stay on the subject and her supply of irrelevant reminiscence. So, messages between Romeo and Juliet are passed on, but only after a lengthy examination of what else is on her mind. In the second half of the play, inevitably, this humorous element fades. She assists in Romeo's wedding-night visit, but then leaves Juliet isolated with her insoluble problem. The Nurse is mainly a sympathetic character, but we may question whether it is right for an adult to encourage her teenage charge in such secret behaviour and then leave her to face the moral consequences.

Friar Lawrence

There are questions to be asked about Friar Lawrence, too. He always speaks wisely: the Nurse in Act 3, Scene 3, is particularly impressed. He is moderate, calm, knowledgeable and sympathetic. However, what he does tends to be much less impressive than what he says. He explains why it is unwise for Romeo and Juliet to marry, then marries them. Why? Is he simply so tender-hearted that he cannot bear to see them suffer? He is party to secret arrangements which, while very understandable for teenagers in love, are not the sort of thing a holy friar should encourage. His final arrangements, complicated and devious, though well-meant, fall apart with Friar John's detention in the plague-house. At least he tries to rescue matters in the end, but even here his treatment of Juliet is ineffective. Yet one feels that Shakespeare is presenting him as a worthy, if perhaps misguided, character. Perhaps he is best seen in terms of his role in the Romeo and Juliet story: one of several characters whose importance depends more on their effect on the love story than on themselves as characters.

The Capulets

Of the two warring families, we see more of the home life of the Capulets than of the Montagues: the feast, with Tybalt (see above) in trouble and an older generation happily reminiscing, gives a real sense of a family gathering. However, there are inconsistencies in Lord and Lady Capulet. Capulet can appear tolerant or the opposite, though his hot temper is always apparent. Lady Capulet's age is a problem: she is 27 in Act 1, Scene 3, but she refers to her 'old age' in Act 5, Scene 3. A constant factor with her is the desire to do everything correctly, to avoid difficult decisions and act conventionally. The main significance of the Capulets lies in their roles as parents: seeking to find a husband for Juliet, bullying their unco-operative daughter, grieving over their dead daughter.

The Montagues

Though the Montagues appear as a family group in the first scene, with Romeo's parents questioning Benvolio about Romeo, they are less distinct as a family than the Capulets. Lady Montague's death barely merits a mention, suggesting our lack of involvement with her as a character. Benvolio is very much cast in the role of 'Romeo's friend' and 'Mercutio's friend'. He is present at some key moments, but does very little: he is the man who listens to Mercutio's jokes or announces his death. Interestingly, he plays no part in Romeo's secret plans. Lord and Lady Montague are simply the enemies of the Capulets, but are not themselves directly involved in the fighting, and Montague shares the grief of the Prince and the Capulets at the end and swears to change.

The Royal Family

The Prince says everything he should: his speech in the first scene insists that the violence stops. Unfortunately he does not act on his words, and in the last scene he admits that he has turned a blind eye to the conflict and has been punished by the loss of two kinsman. These two kinsmen are an interesting comparison. Mercutio (see above) associates with Montagues and is quite prepared to challenge Tybalt, a Capulet. Paris is an associate and would-be son–in–law of the Capulets. Clearly the Royal Family cannot be accused of favouring one side or the other in the feud. Paris, noble and honourable, is seen purely in terms of his relationship with Juliet and, since they have only one short scene together, plus his visit to the tomb, it is not surprising that his character is not strongly drawn.

Act 1, Scene 5

Plot synopsis

Romeo and Juliet meet for the first time at the Capulets' feast. Short episodes with servants and between Capulet and his cousin create the party atmosphere before Romeo sees Juliet and is instantly struck with love. Rosaline is immediately forgotten! The love is returned by Juliet with equal devotion, but it is clear that the Montague/Capulet feud is a barrier to their happiness.

 Juliet My only love sprung from my only hate

(line 135)

After Romeo admits his love to himself, Lord Capulet has to restrain Tybalt from attacking the Montague gate-crasher immediately.

Romeo and Juliet move in a world of their own, isolated from the rest of the party. Romeo and Juliet each inquire of the Nurse who the other one is. Their reactions are similar: they know that the consequences could be fatal, but they cannot escape their love.

Text commentary

Romeo transformed

Romeo's friends believe that seeing other beauties will make him forget Rosaline. They succeed only too well. Let us examine the transformation of Romeo and then the dangers that await him and Juliet.

1 Romeo sees Juliet

Romeo   O, she doth teach the torches to burn bright!
It seems she hangs upon the cheek of night
Like a rich jewel in an Ethiop's ear;
Beauty too rich for use, for earth too dear.
So shows a snowy dove trooping with crows,
As yonder lady o'er her fellows shows.
The measure done, I'll watch her place of stand,
And, touching hers, make blessed my rude hand.
Did my heart love till now? Forswear it, sight!
For I ne'er saw true beauty till this night.

(lines 41–50)

It is important that you notice how sudden the love of Romeo and Juliet is, a perfect example of 'love at first sight'. Romeo's only previous words in this scene are to ask (unsuccessfully) who Juliet is. If you examine what Juliet's first words are, you will find that her reactions are just as speedy. Remember that, when we saw them before, Juliet was claiming to be too young for marriage (Act 1, Scene 3) and Romeo was still lovesick for Rosaline (Act 1, Scene 2) and hopelessly gloomy (Act 1, Scene 4).

 Romeo I'll go along, no such sight to be shown,
But to rejoice in splendour of mine own.

(1.2, lines 98–99)

In this quotation Romeo's 'splendour' is Rosaline. Contrast this with his words in the scene we are studying.

Shakespeare normally writes in either **prose** or **blank verse**. In the first meeting of Romeo and Juliet he constantly uses rhyme, in this speech, rhyming **couplets**. What do you think is the effect of using rhyme? It certainly makes the verse more noticeable. How does that affect our reaction to the speech?

You will have noticed the rich romantic **imagery** in this speech. The most striking **simile** is in lines 42–43. An 'Ethiop' is a black African, so Juliet shines out against the darkness like a precious jewel glittering against a black face. This, of course, fits in with the idea that Juliet's beauty is brighter than the burning torches. See if you can find another simile that suggests that Juliet surpasses all other beauties.

 Romeo For I ne'er saw true beauty till this night.
Tybalt This by his voice should be a Montague.

(lines 50–51)

Though this is a romantic love scene, the hint of **tragedy** is always there. No sooner has Romeo committed himself to love than Tybalt reminds us of the family feud that commits Capulets to hate Romeo.

2 Romeo and Juliet: a love sonnet

Romeo If I profane with my unworthiest hand
This holy shrine, the gentle sin is this,
My lips, two blushing pilgrims, ready stand
To smooth that rough touch with a tender kiss.

Juliet	Good pilgrim, you do wrong your hand too much,
	Which mannerly devotion shows in this;
	For saints have hands that pilgrims' hands do touch,
	And palm to palm is holy palmers' kiss.
Romeo	Have not saints lips, and holy palmers too?
Juliet	Ay, pilgrim, lips that they must use in prayer.
Romeo	O then dear saint, let lips do what hands do.
	They pray; grant thou, lest faith turn to despair.
Juliet	Saints do not move, though grant for prayers' sake.
Romeo	Then move not, while my prayer's effect I take.

(lines 90–103)

In Elizabethan times by far the most popular form of love poem was the sonnet. Poets (including Shakespeare) wrote long sequences of them to their beloveds. By using the **sonnet** form for these first speeches of Romeo and Juliet together, Shakespeare is sending a clear message to the audience or reader. Also the artificial form serves to isolate Romeo and Juliet from their surroundings in a rapturous world of their own. If you were producing the play, how would you stage this scene?

When you plan your essay, make a clear decision about what each paragraph is going to be about. If at all possible, make it clear what the subject or topic of the paragraph is in the first sentence, often called a 'topic sentence'.

This first exchange between Romeo and Juliet leads up to the first kiss, a surprisingly public one. The kiss is seen as a direct result of the poetry: 'You kiss by th'book' (line 107). Just as in any love sonnet, the **imagery** is very important, here based on the **metaphor** of the pilgrim.

A pilgrim was a person who journeyed to a holy place (shrine) to express his or her devotion to some saint or holy person associated with the shrine. For instance, pilgrims travelled to Jerusalem where Christ was crucified or, nearer home, to Canterbury where St

Thomas à Becket was martyred. If Romeo is a pilgrim, then Juliet is a saint and his love is holy devotion. You should note that 'palmer' is an old word for 'pilgrim'. Juliet is able, therefore, to make jokes about pilgrims meeting 'palm to palm'.

 Juliet Then have my lips the sin that they have took?

(line 105)

Juliet frequently says to Romeo that they should not kiss (lines 94–97, for instance). Do you think that she really objects to Romeo's kisses? This quotation certainly sounds like an invitation to him to take his sin again.

See how many words you can find in lines 90–107 that suggest religion and religious belief. The impression is that their love is based on 'devotion' and 'adoration', both words which can be applied to romantic love or to religion. This contrasts with the attitude of the Nurse, who gives a coarse and materialistic motive for marrying Juliet.

 Nurse I tell you, he that can lay hold of her
Shall have the chinks.

(lines 111–112)

The Nurse brings things down to earth: Juliet is a good target for a young suitor because she is rich. Look at the phrasing, full of **slang**: 'lay hold of', 'the chinks'.

3 A love tragedy

 Juliet If he be married,
My grave is like to be my wedding-bed.

Nurse His name is Romeo, and a Montague,
The only son of your great enemy.

Juliet My only love sprung from my only hate,
Too early seen unknown, and known too late!
Prodigious birth of love it is to me,
That I must love a loathed enemy.

(lines 131–138)

There are various ways in which Shakespeare indicates that this love will not be develop happily, but will lead to **tragedy** for the devoted, but doomed, lovers. You might, for instance, like to check what Romeo's feelings are before the feast in Act 1, Scene 4. In this scene, Scene 5, Romeo reacts to discovering Juliet's identity by saying, 'O dear account, my life is my foe's debt' (line 115). In other words, he is at the mercy of his enemy.

Juliet's reaction here is very similar. Her speech contrasts opposites, ending up with the **paradox**: 'I must love a loathed enemy.' Romeo is her enemy, as she was his 'foe' earlier, but there is no choice: she must love him. Look at lines 131–132 before she knows who he is. At this stage she worries about whether he is married and says that if he is it will kill her.

Quotations are useful in an examination essay, but should be kept fairly short. You should quote a line or two, set out on the page as in the text, or fit a few words into your own sentence, identifying the quotation with speech-marks.

Tybalt has to be restrained from drawing his sword on Romeo at the feast simply because he is a Montague, and his words show the depth of hatred between the two families.

| Tybalt | Now by the stock and honour of my kin, |
| | To strike him dead I hold it not a sin. |

(lines 55–56)

Think about the part that will be played in the tragedy by Tybalt's hot temper and hatred of Montagues. Capulet, perhaps surprisingly, is very moderate and tolerant in his comments on Romeo, of whom he has heard good things. His respect for the conventions of hospitality rules out violence to a guest, even a gate-crasher. You will find it useful to compare Capulet's reaction to Tybalt with his reaction to Juliet's refusal to marry Paris in Act 3, Scene 5. He takes a similar approach with both young relations who dare to disagree with him.

Quiz

Can you trace the plot?

By the end of the scene Romeo and Juliet are suddenly, devotedly, in love, unable to live separately, but unable to marry (or even meet) publicly. Trace the events that lead to their brief happiness and later tragedy.

a) Romeo has come to the feast with Benvolio and Mercutio. They expect to leave the party with him. What does he do?

b) The balcony scene (Act 2, Scene 2) is deservedly famous as a love scene, but what precise arrangements do Romeo and Juliet make for the next day?

c) What parts do Friar Lawrence and the Nurse play in the marriage?

d) When Tybalt kills Mercutio, whom does he actually wish to challenge? Why?

e) Why is Romeo so mild towards Tybalt? What is the result of his mildness?

Can you fill in the background?

This scene is mainly to do with Romeo and Juliet's love at first sight, their discovery of each other's identities and the threats of Tybalt, subdued by Capulet. However, there are other elements in the scene; in fact, the first quarter of the scene consists entirely of background action. Try to explain the purpose of these other episodes:

a) At least four servants are involved in the first 13 lines. What is the purpose of this little introduction?

b) When the Capulets enter (line 14), the next 25 lines are devoted to Lord Capulet's speech and his conversation with the other older Capulet. How does this add atmosphere and contrast?

c) What do Capulet's other speeches to the guests (lines 83–85 and 118–124) show about him?

Do you know these words?

Do you know the meaning of these words, all used in Act 1, Scene 5?

a) 'trencher' (line 2)

b) 'banquet' (line 119)

c) 'fay' (line 123)

d) 'antic' (line 53)

e) 'marchpane' (line 7)

f) 'nuptial' (line 33)

g) 'portly' (line 63)

h) 'contrary' (line 82)

i) 'measure' (line 47)

j) 'gall' (line 89)

Sample question

The first meeting between Romeo and Juliet takes place in the middle of a large party. There is an enormous contrast between their discussion and the events that are happening around them. Explain how this contrast is created, looking at:

- *the language used,*
- *the devices that might be used on stage,*
- *the differences between the characters.*

You might find it easier to tackle this essay in two halves, concentrating on the two different sets of events as suggested in the title. Remember, you are being asked to look at the contrasts, so be prepared to point out exactly what the differences are.

The romance When Romeo first sees Juliet, he is unable to think about anything else. Which of the rich images he uses suggest that she is more than just a girl? This helps to create an atmosphere that is calm and gentle. How else does Shakespeare emphasise this feeling? How does Juliet react to Romeo?

The excitement of the party Look at the preparations, with the servants rushing around, and the way Capulet speaks to his guests as they arrive. Pick out lines that suggest Capulet's good humour and the sense of warmth and welcome.

The danger Tybalt is deeply insulted when he realises that a Montague has come to his uncle's house. He wants revenge. How does Shakespeare give the impression that even Capulet has difficulty in controlling him? How does he show his violent nature? Why is this confrontation important later in the play?

Time There are two different time scales in the scene. The party is all noise and bustle and everything seems to rush along. The discussion between Romeo and Juliet seems completely separate from it, as though time stands still. At the same time, the moment they kiss they are interrupted by the real world. These differences are apparent in the language that is used, but a director would find other ways of pointing them out to the audience. How might lighting be used and music? The positions of characters on stage may be important. What other devices might be used on film, such as the position of the camera or the type of shot?

Think about some of the things that happen before and after this scene that support the contrasts you have been pointing out. Just before the party, Romeo says:

> 'My mind misgives
> Some consequence, yet hanging in the stars'
>
> *(lines 106–107)*

What does he mean by this? What difference does it make to what the audience expects when he meets Juliet? Consider, also, what happens next time he meets Tybalt.

ACT 2, SCENES 4 AND 5

Plot synopsis

After some mocking of the lovelorn Romeo by Benvolio and, especially, Mercutio, these scenes consist of three conversations involving the Nurse, separated by a single speech from Juliet. In the first conversation the Nurse is subjected to offensive humour, much of it sexual, by Mercutio. In the second, she is alone with Romeo and receives his instructions about the marriage. Juliet, meanwhile, is consumed with impatience:

| Juliet | Had she affections and warm youthful blood, |
| | She would be swift in motion as a ball. |

(2.5, lines 12–13)

Once she arrives, the Nurse is slow getting to the point and has trouble staying on it. Eventually, however, Juliet hears what she has hoped for.

| Nurse | Then hie you hence to Friar Lawrence's cell, |
| | There stays a husband to make you a wife. |

(2.5, lines 67–68)

Text commentary

The Nurse as messenger

 These scenes are dominated by the activities of the Nurse as go-between, and both contain much humour. We are now going to compare two sections where the Nurse delivers messages, one where Juliet reveals the state of her feelings.

1 The Nurse and Romeo

| Romeo | Farewell, be trusty, and I'll quit thy pains. |
| | Farewell, commend me to thy mistress. |

| Nurse | Now God in heaven bless thee. Hark you, sir. |

| Romeo | What sayest thou, my dear Nurse? |

| Nurse | Is your man secret? Did you ne'er hear say, |
| | Two may keep counsel, putting one away? |

| Romeo | I warrant thee my man's as true as steel. |

> *Nurse*   Well, sir, my mistress is the sweetest lady. Lord,
> Lord, when 'twas a little prating thing. O there is a
> nobleman in town, one Paris, that would fain lay
> knife aboard; but she, good soul, had as lief see a
> toad, a very toad, as see him. I anger her
> sometimes, and tell her Paris is the properer man;
> but I'll warrant you when I say so, she looks as pale
> as any clout in the versal world. Doth not rosemary
> and Romeo begin both with a letter?
>
> *(2.4, lines 173–186)*

Romeo has just given the Nurse instructions. Juliet must make the excuse of confession to go to Friar Lawrence's cell to be married this very afternoon. The Nurse must work with Romeo's servant to provide him with a rope-ladder to let him into Juliet's bedroom for a secret wedding night. The Nurse is taking this very seriously: she wonders whether Romeo's servant is to be trusted. You may well be amused at the Nurse claiming that someone else may be unable to keep a secret. Her own love of gossip is evident even in this scene. How good, in fact, is her record of keeping Juliet's and Romeo's secrets?

> *Romeo*   What wilt thou tell her, Nurse? Thou dost not mark
> me.
>
> *Nurse*   I will tell her, sir, that you do protest which, as I
> take it, is a gentlemanlike offer.
>
> *(2.4, lines 157–159)*

How do these lines show that the Nurse does not follow what Romeo is actually saying, but understands the essential point he is making?

It takes Romeo a long time to make the Nurse concentrate. Now (from line 160 onwards) her concentration lasts just long enough. The change from serious business to gossip is marked by the change to **prose**. The speech beginning, 'Well, sir, my mistress is the sweetest lady' is amusing, as she changes subject rapidly, and it also reveals much about the Nurse's character. What does it tell us of her relationship with Juliet? What do we learn of the Nurse's education? What does it tell us of her consistency of opinion?

| Nurse | I think it best you married with the County (Paris) ... |
| | Romeo's a dishclout to him. |

(3.5, lines 218 and 220)

What are we to make of the change of mind? There is even a reminder of the same word ('clout' meaning 'cloth') to link the speeches together.

> Examiners know that you are writing against the clock and understand that there will be some errors of spelling, punctuation, etc. However, if you have time, it is always worthwhile to check your completed work thoroughly to reduce mistakes to a minimum.

2 Juliet waits for the Nurse

Juliet	The clock struck nine when I did send the Nurse;
	In half an hour she promised to return.
	Perchance she cannot meet him – that's not so –
	O she is lame, love's heralds should be thought,
	Which ten times faster glides than the sun's beams,
	Driving back shadows over lowering hills.
	Therefore do nimble-pinioned doves draw love,
	And therefore hath the wind-swift Cupid wings.
	Now is the sun upon the highmost hill
	Of this day's journey, and from nine to twelve
	Is three long hours, yet she is not come.

(2.5, lines 1–11)

These scenes are very cleverly written in terms of time. Throughout we feel that there are two different speeds operating, that of the Nurse and that of the lovers. Our impression is of terrible impatience as time passes, yet not very much time has passed. Romeo and Juliet met last night; it is now midday; this afternoon they will be married; tonight he will climb the ladder to her bedroom. This pace is partly created by moving straight from the Nurse leaving Romeo to the Nurse returning to Juliet, with just a pause for this tremulously impatient **soliloquy** by Juliet.

Let us look at Juliet's view of time in the soliloquy. Partly it is very practical, full of time-checks. The audience can thus imagine her impatience, but see that in real terms not much time has passed. The other presentation of time is romantic and comparative. See what **imagery** you can find of love and time, suggesting that in love time must fly. The other key image, of light and shadow, is linked with both time and love. Juliet talks of 'the sun upon the highmost hill'. What image of the delights of love (at the end of this scene) reminds us of this?

The comparison is between youth and age, suggesting that time is both fixed (as on a clock) and flexible (as in our impression of it).

| Juliet | But old folk, many feign as they were dead, |
| | Unwieldy, slow, heavy and pale as lead. |

(lines 16–17)

When the Nurse enters, she justifies this completely in a very funny short scene which is also the introduction to the marriage. Note that the marriage happens in accelerated time, suited to the impatient lovers: Juliet leaves the Nurse in the house at the end of Scene 5 and is embracing Romeo at Friar Lawrence's 15 lines later!

3 The Nurse and Juliet

Nurse	Your love says, like an honest gentleman, and a courteous, and a kind, and a handsome, and I warrant you a virtuous – Where is your mother?
Juliet	Where is my mother? Why, she is within. Where should she be? How oddly thou repliest. 'Your love says like an honest gentleman, "Where is your mother?" '
Nurse	O God's lady dear, Are you so hot? Marry, come up, I trow, Is this the poultice for my aching bones? Henceforward do your messages yourself.
Juliet	Here's such a coil! Come, what says Romeo?
Nurse	Have you got leave to go to shrift today?

(2.5, lines 54-64)

This scene is comic, as are several in the first half of the play. Think of how it should be staged in terms of the positions and actions of the Nurse and Juliet. Also you should consider just how worried Juliet really is. She is impatient for details, certainly, but does she have any real doubt that the Nurse brings good news? On the Nurse's side, do you think that she is really too out of breath and too aggrieved to speak or is it all a friendly game?

In normal circumstances you should use formal correct English, avoiding slang and contractions (e.g. 'they've' for 'they have'). If you are writing in character, this will, of course, change, but clarity of expression is still the most important consideration.

Let us compare the Nurse's time-wasting in this scene and in the previous scene with Romeo. A particularly humorous effect is of the Nurse continually interrupting herself ('Where is your mother?' in line 60). Similar things happen when she is speaking to Romeo, with her interrupting him before he has reached the point. Failing to stay on the subject is the main feature of her conversation. Suddenly asking Romeo about the letter R, or asking Juliet if she has dined at home are good examples: see what others you can find.

 Nurse   Lord, how my head aches, what a head have I!

(line 47)

The other comic form of delay is when the Nurse spends her time bemoaning the effort it has taken to get the message, rather than passing on the message. The speech beginning on line 47 is full of vivid phrases describing her weariness. You could compare this to her complaints about Mercutio upsetting her in the earlier scene with Romeo.

Shakespeare uses the comedy to create a mood of light-heartedness in which Juliet's eager anticipation of the joys of marriage seems unclouded (for the moment) by worries about Romeo's family. The Nurse's final speech and Juliet's words are full of a delighted **pun** on 'hie' (go quickly) and 'high' (the best and also Juliet's high balcony). The Nurse's words effectively combine romantic **imagery** ('climb a bird's nest') with down-to-earth sexual jokes.

| Nurse | I am the drudge, and toil in your delight, |
| | But you shall bear the burden soon at night. |

(2.5, lines 74–75)

Quiz

Can you trace the character?

These scenes are linked by the actions of the Nurse. What effect do her actions throughout the play have on the progress of Romeo and Juliet's love?

a) In Act 1, Scene 3, Lady Capulet encourages Juliet to look with favour on Paris. What role does the Nurse play in this dialogue?

b) The Nurse is actively involved as go-between in these scenes. How has she already introduced Romeo and Juliet to each other?

c) The Nurse brings news of Tybalt's death and Romeo's banishment in Act 3, Scene 2. What 'comfort' does she bring Juliet?

d) What 'comfort' does she fail to give Juliet in Act 3, Scene 5?

e) What part does the Nurse play in Juliet's apparent suicide?

How does the relationship between the Nurse and Juliet change during the play?

Can you finish the sentence?

The Nurse frequently changes the subject between, or in the middle of, sentences. Can you find the following sentences and discover what comes next?

a) 'He is not the flower of courtesy, but I'll warrant him as gentle as a lamb ...'

b) 'I anger her sometimes, and tell her that Paris is the properer man; but I'll warrant you when I say so, she looks as pale as any clout in the versal world ...'

c) 'Your love says, like an honest gentleman, and a courteous, and a kind, and a handsome, and I warrant a virtuous ...'

Do you know these words?

Do you know the meaning of these words, all used in Act 2, Scenes 4 and 5?

a) 'nimble-pinioned' (2.5, line 7)

b) 'coil' (2.5, line 64)

c) 'jauncing' (2.5., line 51)

d) 'flirt-gills' (2.4, line 137)

e) 'shrift' (2.4, line 161)

f) 'perchance' (2.5, line 3)

g) 'wanton' (2.5, line 69)

h) 'hie' (2.5, line 67)

i) 'lief' (2.4, line 182)

j) 'versal' (2.4, line 185)

Sample question

Explain how and why comic and serious events are combined in these scenes. You will need to look at:

- *the role of the nurse,*
- *the plans for the wedding,*
- *Romeo and Juliet's mood,*
- *the secrecy which surrounds their plans.*

In your introduction, you will need to explain that the majority of each scene is funny. Only Romeo and Juliet's plans to marry, their desperation to be together and the need for secrecy are serious.

Although the role of the Nurse does have a serious purpose, she is mainly a comic figure, there to remind us that life is not always dangerous and frightening. The humour here has several sources. Look at and explain the way Romeo's friends react to the Nurse, the things she says to Romeo, the way she tries to act more like a lady than a nurse, the way she delays telling Juliet what she wants to hear and the language that she uses in her speeches. What appears to be her greatest concern in life? How does this compare with others in the play?

The plans for the wedding reveal different sides to the characters of both Romeo and Juliet. Think about ways in which are they similar and ways in which are they different.

What kind of atmosphere is created in these scenes? Is it nervous, excited, light-hearted, reckless? How does Shakespeare create this atmosphere, and why? Try to quote specific parts of the text which prove your point. Look for places where the feelings shift. Look at such lines as:

> 'In half an hour she promised to return.
> Perchance she cannot meet him – that's not so –'

> *(lines 2–3)*

We are reminded that the situation they are in is very dangerous. Look for indications that it must be kept secret, that everything is done in a hurry, that neither of them is in complete control. What effect does this have on the audience? Do we know anything that they don't? In what way are our feelings different from theirs? Only the three of them know of their plans – consider what happens later in the play as a consequence of this.

In your conclusion, say a little about how this scene fits into the rest of the play. Think about how many other scenes contain this amount of comedy. Why do you think Shakespeare chose to present this scene in particular in this way?

Act 3, Scene 2

Plot synopsis

Juliet, alone, thinks of the coming of night and, therefore, of Romeo. She is totally unaware of the brawl, the death of Tybalt and Romeo's banishment. Her speech anticipates the delights of her wedding night. The Nurse enters, but is so distraught that Juliet finds her message confusing.

 Juliet   Is Romeo slaughtered? And is Tybalt dead?
My dearest cousin, and my dearer lord?

(lines 65–66)

Juliet undergoes a whole range of emotions, but ultimately remains loyal to Romeo. She makes it clear that Tybalt's death, though sad, is much less of a cause for grief than Romeo's banishment. Juliet expects to die a maid, but the Nurse offers final consolation by offering to bring Romeo from Friar Lawrence's cell that night.

Text commentary

Juliet's hopes shattered

Act 3, Scenes 1 and 2, turn round the plot of the play. Hitherto Romeo and Juliet's love, though faced with difficulties, has made good progress: they are both full of optimism. In these two scenes Romeo, then Juliet, have their dreams destroyed before, at last, finding hope of celebrating their wedding night.

1 Juliet dreams of night

 Juliet   Gallop apace, you fiery-footed steeds,
Towards Phoebus' lodging; such a wagoner
As Phaeton would whip you to the west,
And bring in cloudy night immediately.
Spread thy close curtain, love-performing night,
That runaway's eyes may wink, and Romeo

Leap to these arms, untalked of and unseen.
Lovers can see to do their amorous rites
By their own beauties; or if love be blind,
It best agrees with night. Come civil night,
Thou sober-suited matron all in black,
And learn me how to lose a winning match,
Played for a pair of stainless maidenhoods.

(lines 1–13)

The opening of the scene makes a telling comparison with Act 2, Scene 5. In both Juliet is impatient for the return of the Nurse and for the presence of Romeo. In the earlier scene, Juliet has doubts, not about the love of Romeo, but about why the Nurse is so late. When the Nurse arrives, after much comic delay and misunderstanding, she gives Juliet good news. In this case, Juliet feels no doubt, but the news the Nurse brings could hardly be worse. Just as in Act 2, Scene 5, it takes a long time for the Nurse to communicate her information, but there is nothing comic this time.

 Timing your test essays is important. As the test proceeds, check your progress against the clock in the room. Make sure that you are giving yourself enough time to finish, but also check that you are not progressing too rapidly. If you finish very early, you have not included enough detail, so, if you realise this is going to happen, develop your arguments at greater length and add more references and quotations. Finishing 5–10 minutes early is a good idea, leaving time to check your work.

This opening speech conveys the rapture of young love better than any other part of the play. Note the various devices that Shakespeare uses. Mostly it consists of an appeal to Night; addressing the **personification** of Night gives the speech the tone of an intense declamation. Night is personified in contrasting form, as 'love-performing' and 'thou sober-suited matron'.

The opening cry is even more intense and dramatic, with an appeal to the horses of the sun. Phoebus was the sun-god in Roman **mythology**, and Phaeton was his son. Phoebus drove his horses through the sky and, at sunset, lodged them for the night. Phaeton obtained permission to drive the chariot, rushed madly out of control and had to be struck down by Jupiter, the supreme god. What impression is given at this time by such a tale of disaster befalling impetuous youth?

Later in the speech Juliet addresses Romeo and applies some striking **imagery** to him.

| Juliet | For thou wilt lie upon the wings of night, |
| | Whiter than new snow upon a raven's back. |

(lines 18–19)

The **simile** suggests purity, as does 'stainless maidenhoods' in line 13. There is passion and desire, but also something holy about Juliet's love. Lovers perform 'amorous rites' (line 8), rites being ceremonies such as might be part of a religious celebration. What is the effect of calling Romeo 'thou day in night' (line 17) and talking of cutting him out 'in little stars' (line 22)?

2 Making sense of the Nurse

Nurse	Alack the day, he's gone, he's killed, he's dead.
Juliet	Can heaven be so envious?
Nurse	Romeo can,
	Though heaven cannot. O Romeo, Romeo,
	Whoever would have thought it? Romeo!

(lines 39–42)

Juliet	Vile earth, to earth resign; end motion here;
	And thou and Romeo press one heavy bier.
Nurse	O Tybalt, Tybalt, the best friend I had,
	O courteous Tybalt, honest gentleman,
	That ever I should live to see thee dead!
Juliet	What storm is this that blows so contrary?
	Is Romeo slaughtered? And is Tybalt dead?

(lines 59-65)

34

The similarities to, and differences from, Act 2, Scene 5, are touching. In the earlier scene the Nurse enjoys her gossip and her complaints and is probably teasing Juliet deliberately. Now the delays and confusion are just as great and partly for the same reason, that the Nurse cannot stay on the subject, but now it is her grief that drives her to mention a name without explaining why. It takes over 30 lines for the Nurse to tell Juliet what has happened. How do you think Juliet's feelings here compare with Act 2, Scene 5, when she is also trying to obtain information?

At the end of a test essay it is useful to sum up your opinions with a conclusion. However, it is more important to keep your main argument in view throughout, and simply repeating yourself in a lengthy concluding paragraph gains little credit.

The Nurse specialises in the irrelevant and confusing. However, in one sense, she gets to the point immediately. In line 37 she says, 'We are undone', meaning that she and Juliet are ruined. What exactly is she referring to? How is she ruined?

Juliet's reaction to the thought that Romeo has killed himself is that the news is deadly poison to her (lines 46–47) and she abandons all thought of life and wishes to share a 'heavy bier' with Romeo. This shows the intensity of her feelings and serves as a prophecy of later events.

As an audience we only see Tybalt as a brash bully-boy, bringing disaster to his cousin and her secret husband, rejecting Romeo's peace offers, stabbing Mercutio in what might be seen as a foul blow. Look here at what the Nurse has to say about him: to someone, at least, he was courteous, honest and a good friend. What do we learn of Juliet's feelings about him?

3 Juliet rages

Juliet   O serpent heart, hid with a flow'ring face!
               Did ever dragon keep so fair a cave?

> Beautiful tyrant, fiend angelical,
> Dove-feathered raven, wolfish-ravening lamb,
> Despised substance of divinest show,
> Just opposite to what thou justly seem'st,
> A damned saint, an honourable villain.

(lines 73–79)

As Juliet finally realises what has happened, she becomes temporarily unbalanced. Her feelings towards Romeo are contradictory. He still seems as fair as ever to her, but briefly she also sees him as treacherous and evil. Shakespeare brings out the fractured nature of Juliet's thoughts by using a series of **oxymorons**. Particularly good examples are 'fiend angelical', where he is described as a devil and an angel, and the very similar 'damned saint'. See what other examples of oxymorons you can find in these seven lines.

Juliet	Blistered be thy tongue
	For such a wish. He was not born to shame.

(lines 90–91)

Soon Juliet recovers her faith in Romeo. One reason for this is that the Nurse too readily joins in blaming Romeo: 'Shame come to Romeo' (line 90). Juliet's response is predictably fierce and protective. Juliet is, in a sense, right to assume that Romeo was defending himself against an attack from Tybalt (line 101), though it was more complicated than that. However, her interpretation of events is based as much on loyalty and love as on evidence.

Juliet   Shall I speak ill of him that is my husband?

(line 97)

4 Juliet grieves for Romeo

Juliet   Some word there was, worser than Tybalt's death,
That murdered me. I would forget it fain;
But o it presses to my memory,
Like damned guilty deeds to sinners' minds.
'Tybalt is dead, and Romeo banished.'
That 'banished', that one word 'banished',
Hath slain ten thousand Tybalts.

(lines 108–114)

Throughout this speech, which continues in similar style for some 12 lines more, Juliet constantly manipulates the same few words: 'dead' (and words of similar meaning), 'banished', 'Romeo', 'Tybalt' (and, later, her parents as well). The effect of the variations on these words is to express that the banishment of Romeo brings greater grief than the death of any of her other loved ones. Notice how Juliet uses 'death' words to make this point. The news of banishment 'murdered' her and 'hath slain ten thousand Tybalts'. This means that her grief for Tybalt's death is only one ten-thousandth of her grief for Romeo's banishment.

You should be able to make sure that you finish your essay in the test. However, if you run out of time before you have made all the points you want to, spend the last five minutes jotting down in note form what you intended to write. It is not ideal, but it is better than leaving them out altogether.

This speech also contains a subtle and extended use of **alliteration**. Besides death and banishment, there is a series of words beginning with 'w', linking together the grief and its causes: 'weep', 'woe', 'worser' and, above all, 'word' (the word in question being 'banished'). The effect of this pattern of words is to give the impression of Juliet being totally obsessed with Romeo's banishment, beyond all other woes that she could weep for, like Tybalt's death. The pattern is completed with the Nurse's reply to her question about her mother and father: 'Weeping and wailing over Tybalt's corse' (line 128).

> *Juliet*   Come cords, come Nurse, I'll to my wedding-bed,
> And death, not Romeo, take my maidenhead.
>
> *(lines 136–137)*

The scene ends with the Nurse planning to bring Romeo to Juliet, but the dominant image of the scene is still death.

Quiz

Can you trace the plot?

Romeo and Juliet have one intention throughout the scenes following their secret marriage: to consummate their marriage that night. So great is their anticipation of joy that they feel no enmity towards others. However, between the ceremony and the wedding night (that is, in the first four scenes of Act 3), many people's actions destroy their happiness.

a) What does Tybalt want to see Romeo for in Act 3, Scene 1? How does Romeo react, and why?

b) What prompts Mercutio's actions in the same scene? How do they affect Romeo?

c) What verdict does the Prince reach, and why?

d) What effect does Capulet think Tybalt's death has had on Paris' hopes of wooing Juliet (Act 3, Scene 4)?

e) What change of policy does he therefore decide on?

Can you compare the scenes?

a) Juliet constantly speaks of banishment as being death or worse than death. So does Romeo in conversation with Friar Lawrence in the next scene (Act 3, Scene 3). Find at least six occasions between lines 4 and 70 where Romeo links banishment and death.

b) In lines 101–107 Juliet tries to find consolation in the fact that Tybalt failed to kill her husband. In Act 3, Scene 3, the Friar spends lines 135–154 trying to console Romeo. What reasons does he find?

c) The commentary pointed out certain key words that Juliet uses repeatedly in this scene. In lines 84–102 of Act 3, Scene 3, the Nurse repeats some of them. Can you find them?

Do you know these words?

Do you know the meaning of these words, all used in Act 3, Scene 2?

a) 'wot' (line 139)

b) 'modern' (line 120)

c) 'unmanned' (line 14)

d) 'cockatrice' (line 47)

e) 'rear-ward' (line 121)

f) 'dissemblers' (line 87)

g) 'bier' (line 60)

h) 'wagoner' (line 2)

i) 'undone' (line 38)

j) 'aqua vitae' (line 48)

Sample question

Write an explanation of the way Juliet feels in this scene. How much do you sympathise with her situation? You will need to look at:

- *her relationship with her parents, with Tybalt and with Romeo,*
- *how the way she speaks reflects the way she feels,*
- *how the presence of the nurse contributes to the scene,*
- *the way Shakespeare shows how confused Juliet feels.*

What is your impression of Juliet in this scene? Is she an immature teenager who can't cope with real life, or is she a passionate woman with good reason to be distressed? Does she behave differently in this scene, compared with her earlier appearances? Juliet's relationship with her parents is an important factor. She cannot share the way she feels with them because they don't know about Romeo. Why has Juliet not told them, or are her parents so different from her that they could never understand? Remember, Juliet also has no one else dependable she can rely on for advice. How does the Nurse show her unreliability in this scene?

The scene opens with Juliet wishing night would come, waiting for Romeo to arrive so that they can spend their wedding night together. Pick out particular words and phrases that show how Juliet feels.

When the Nurse breaks the news to Juliet, she adds to the tension in the scene by, at first, making Juliet think that Romeo is dead, and then that both he and Tybalt have been killed. This means that Juliet's emotions change very quickly, while the audience already knows exactly what has happened. How does the nurse feel in the scene, and how is it different from the way Juliet feels? How does she talk about Tybalt? The nurse has helped Romeo and Juliet marry. Is she also to blame?

The key speech in this scene is the one beginning on line 97 'Shall I speak ill of him ...'. Look carefully at this speech. How does Juliet persuade herself not to think badly of Romeo? Look at some of the contrasts and contradictions near the beginning which help to show how confused she feels – she speaks of comfort and weeping, she calls Romeo and Tybalt villain in turn, and so on. How has Juliet changed by the end of the speech?

Look at the following phrases:

'Blistered be thy tongue' (line 90),

'This torture should be roared in dismal hell.' (line 44)

'What storm is this that blows so contrary?' (line 64)

There are many lines in the scene that suggest pain, violence and conflict. Find other examples. What impression do they give of Juliet and of her relationship with Romeo? Are there other times when similar suggestions are made?.

Juliet begins the scene full of hope and expectation and ends it full of despair. Where else in the play do similar changes take place? Why are they included? You might like to look back at the prologue, in particular to lines such as 'The fearful passage of their death-marked love'.

ACT 3, SCENE 5

Plot synopsis

Before this scene starts, Juliet's happiness is already doomed. She has married Romeo who has slain Tybalt and must flee to Mantua. Now her father is planning for her to marry Paris. At the beginning of the scene Romeo leaves reluctantly on the morning after their wedding night. Lady Capulet misunderstands Juliet's grief and thinks that she is mourning for Tybalt. When she tells Juliet of the planned marriage to Paris, Juliet refuses to co-operate.

41

| | Juliet | Now by St. Peter's Church, and Peter too,
He shall not make me there a joyful bride. |

(lines 116–117)

Lord Capulet enters and threatens to disown Juliet if she opposes the plan. Finally Juliet turns for assistance to the Nurse who also lets her down by suggesting that she should forget all about Romeo and marry Paris. Deserted by mother, father and nurse, Juliet is left to think that death might be the only way out.

Text commentary

Juliet's problems

Let us examine four passages of text that show Juliet's relationships with the other characters and reveal her impossible dilemma.

1 Juliet and Romeo

| | Juliet | Wilt thou be gone? It is not yet near day.
It was the nightingale, and not the lark,
That pierced the fearful hollow of thine ear;
Nightly she sings on yon pomegranate tree.
Believe me, love, it was the nightingale. |
| | Romeo | It was the lark, the herald of the morn,
No nightingale. Look, love, what envious streaks
Do lace the severing clouds in yonder east.
Night's candles are burnt out, and jocund day
Stands tiptoe on the misty mountain tops. |

(lines 1–10)

Take a careful note of the **imagery** in this dialogue. Though the topic of conversation is the need to flee to escape capture and death, it is full of poetic suggestions of nature: lark, nightingale, pomegranate tree. There is **personification** of the times of day. 'Jocund' (cheerful) day is standing ready to appear (lines 9–10). Find examples of how the dawn and night are personified.

 Romeo   I must be gone and live, or stay and die.

(line 11)

The opening section has to convince us of Romeo and Juliet's love and happiness together as well as their danger. They express themselves in romantic, poetic terms, and regularly call each other 'love'. This means far more than it does the way it is used today (like 'dear' or 'darling'). It actually means 'Love': look back to the Balcony Scene, Act 2, Scene 2, line 50.

Do you think that Juliet really believes that is still night? Soon (line 26) she changes her mind about the lark. Why do you think that she insists at first that it is the nightingale?

 Before an examination, make sure that you revise the whole text. You will be concentrating particularly on one scene, but you will also need to make reference to other parts of the play.

 Juliet   O God, I have an ill-divining soul!

(line 54)

Although Romeo is apparently about to escape and she does not yet know about the planned marriage to Paris, Juliet fears the worst and anticipates tragedy.

2 Juliet and her mother

Lady Capulet   Marry, my child, early next Thursday morn,
                The gallant, young and noble gentleman,
                The County Paris, at St. Peter's Church,
                Shall happily make thee there a joyful bride.

Juliet	Now by St. Peter's Church, and Peter too,
	He shall not make me there a joyful bride.
	I wonder at this haste, that I must wed
	Ere he that should be husband comes to woo.
	I pray you tell my lord and father, madam,
	I will not marry yet, and, when I do, I swear
	It shall be Romeo, whom you know I hate,
	Rather than Paris.

(lines 112–123)

Let us think about what this shows about Juliet's relationship with her mother. They are not angry with each other, they do not wish each other harm, but how close are they to each other? We can find many examples of **formality** in speech, rather than affection. Look at the sort of terms Lady Capulet uses about Paris, or Juliet uses about her father.

Lady Capulet	I would the fool were married to her grave!

(line 140)

Do as thou wilt, for I have done with thee.

(line 204)

Why do you think Lady Capulet's coldness turns to such cruel anger later in the scene?

In the examination you will have a copy of the scene in front of you to remind you of any quotation you need. However, it is worth learning key quotations. Examinations are against the clock and it helps to know what quotations you are looking for and where they are to be found.

The conversation in lines 112–123 proceeds by opposites. The best example is probably where Juliet repeats her mother's lines (114–115) with opposite meaning. Juliet's statements, 'he that should be husband' and 'I swear it shall be Romeo ... Rather than Paris' have opposite meanings to speaker and listener. Make sure that you understand how Juliet manages to speak the truth without offending her mother.

Juliet	Villain and he are many miles asunder.

(line 81)

This is an example of another way in which Juliet can tell truth: by using an **aside**. Juliet is here concerned with truth and honour, being true to her own nature and also to her vows. Her mother's concern with family and status does not relate to her at all. Lady Capulet's 'tell him so yourself' may strike you as typical of many mothers dealing with teenagers, but the fury that bursts from Lord Capulet astonishes everyone, including his wife.

3 Juliet and her father

Juliet   Not proud you have, but thankful that you have.
            Proud can I never be of what I hate,
            But thankful even for hate, that is meant love.

Capulet How, how, how, how, chopt-logic. What is this?
            'Proud' and 'I thank you' and 'I thank you not',
            And yet 'not proud'. Mistress minion you,
            Thank me no thankings, nor proud me no prouds,
            But fettle your fine joints 'gainst Thursday next,
            To go with Paris to St. Peter's Church,
            Or I will drag thee on a hurdle thither.
            Out you green-sickness carrion, out you baggage,
            You tallow-face!

(lines 146–157)

Juliet attempts the sort of **wordplay** that she used with her mother, only to be accused of being a 'chopt-logic', one who uses apparently logical views to create an argument. Capulet shows his feelings openly and declares his authority and power over his daughter. His language is offensive enough here, but you can find even more shocking examples later.

Capulet Hang thee, young baggage, disobedient wretch!

(line 160)

And you be mine, I'll give you to my friend;
And you be not, hang, beg, starve, die in the streets.

(lines 192–93)

Make a list of the violent and explosive **monosyllables** that Capulet hurls at his daughter.

In contrast to the rather formal speech of his wife, note Capulet's use of **slang** and **colloquialisms**. Among the colloquial insults he applies to Juliet are 'mistress minion' (spoilt girl), 'green-sickness carrion' (the anaemic corpse of a young girl) and 'baggage' (good-for-nothing female). See what other similar insults you can find in lines 176-196.

Do you think that Capulet really means his threats? Would he really carry Juliet to church on a hurdle, for instance? Juliet is understandably terrified. Her mother fails to support her. At least the Nurse tries to interrupt on her behalf (lines 168-70). Surely she will help!

4 Juliet and the Nurse

Juliet   Some comfort, nurse.

Nurse   Faith, here it is. Romeo
Is banished, and all the world to nothing,
That he dares ne'er to come back to challenge you;
Or if he do, it needs must be by stealth.
Then since the case so stands as now it doth,
I think it best you married with the County.
O he's a lovely gentleman.
Romeo's a dishclout to him; an eagle, madam,
Hath not so green, so quick, so fair an eye
As Paris hath. Beshrew my very heart,
I think you are happy in this second match,
For it exceeds your first; or if it did not,
Your first is dead, or 'twere as good he were,
As living hence, and you no use to him.

(lines 213–226)

Juliet seeks 'comfort': she uses the word three times in her conversation with the Nurse. However, the comfort that Juliet seeks and the comfort that the Nurse tries to give are totally different.

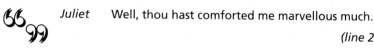   *Juliet*   Well, thou hast comforted me marvellous much.

(line 229)

This line is **ironic**. The Nurse's comfort consists of telling Juliet that Romeo will not come back and Paris is finer and more handsome than Romeo. What sort of 'comfort' was Juliet hoping for?

Juliet objects to the Nurse's speech on two grounds. First of all she resents the way in which she 'dispraises' Romeo (line 236). Re-read what the Nurse said about Romeo in Act 2, Scene 5, and compare it with what she is saying now. Why has she changed so much?

> Nurse an honest gentleman,
> And a courteous, and a kind, and a handsome ...
>
> *(2.5, lines 54–55)*
>
> Romeo's a dishclout to him   *(3.5, line 220)*

Juliet's second objection is the Nurse's lack of moral guidance. She has no objection to bigamy (marrying more than once) so long as nobody knows about it. The Nurse twice uses the word 'beshrew' (curse) applied to her heart and soul. In view of her encouragement to sin, this is very appropriate.

You will have long enough in your tests to prepare the essay properly. Use the reading time sensibly by deciding what are the main points you need for your essay, making a list of them and planning in what order you are going to deal with them.

Quiz

Can you trace the plot?

Juliet has been let down by her parents and her nurse. At the end of this scene she decides that she must look elsewhere for help.

a) Whom does she choose to help her? Find a quotation from this scene.

b) What does he do to help her?

c) What do they expect to happen as a result of their actions?

d) What actually happens?

e) What is the most important reason why things turn out differently from the plan?

Can you identify this image?

Imagery of day and night is a crucial part of the way in which the love of Romeo and Juliet is expressed. The opening of this scene is a good example. So, too, are Act 2, Scene 2, and Act 3, Scene 2. What do the following images in those scenes refer to?

a) 'Gallop apace, you fiery-footed steeds,/Towards Phoebus' lodging' (3.2, lines 1–2)
b) 'Thou sober-suited matron all in black' (3.2, line 11)
c) 'It is the east ...' (2.2, line 3)
d) 'The brightness of her cheek would shame those stars' (2.2, line 19)
e) 'Whiter than new snow upon a raven's back' (3.2, line 19)

Do you know these words?

Do you know the meaning of these words, all used in Act 3, Scene 5?

a) 'affray' (line 33)
b) 'division' (line 29)
c) 'conduit' (line 129)
d) 'counsellor' (line 238)
e) 'dishclout' (line 220)
f) 'mammet' (line 185)
g) 'runagate' (line 89)
h) 'ill-divining' (line 54)
i) 'demesnes' (line 181)
j) 'nobly liened' (line 181)

Sample question

What do you consider to be the most dramatic elements in this scene?

- *You should remember that what happens here has an important effect on what happens later.*
- *Who do you think bears most responsibility for the break down in relationships?*
- *Think about the way contrasting atmospheres are created at different points.*
- *Look at how relationships between characters change.*

In your introduction, place the question in context by briefly outlining what has led to Juliet finding herself in this predicament and what happens afterwards because of it. This will help you explain the importance of the scene.

Next, use the bullet points or question advice to structure your essay by dealing with each of the relationships that are portrayed in the scene. A lot of the drama comes from the contrast between them. We begin by seeing the obvious happiness of Romeo and Juliet, but even here there are tensions and hints that there is more unhappiness to follow. Find examples of this and explain their effect on the audience.

Contrast this with the violence of the argument between Capulet and Juliet, when he tells her to 'hang, beg, starve, die on the streets.' Find other examples of Capulet's violent language and use them to explain how he feels about Juliet's refusal and why. Find other examples of contrasts between the two parts of the scene, such as gentleness and savagery (look at different animals that are mentioned), love and hate, hope and despair. It is the speed with which we move from one to the other that makes the scene so powerful.

Juliet and her mother never seem close in the play, but here they have become very distant, though only Juliet realises by just how much. Study the conversation between them and explain some of the ways Juliet deliberately misleads her mother. Contrast Juliet's gentle views of Romeo with her mother's violent plans. Why is Lady Capulet so keen to see Juliet married to Paris? Is she surprised by Juliet's reaction, and if so, why?

Juliet's relationship with the Nurse is transformed in this scene. How and why? What does this tell us about Juliet?

Considering which of the characters you blame most for the events in this scene is a good way to end your essay, because you can sum up a lot of the points you've already made and use them as evidence to back up your views. However, remember that with this kind of question you must look at all the characters rather than just one, including those who contribute but are not actually there.

Since this question is specifically about dramatic elements, you might mention some of the techniques that could be used to bring out the most important moments. For example, when Juliet and her father argue, where do they stand? How would you give the impression of the power the one has over the other? What are Juliet's mother and the Nurse doing?

In the final few lines of the essay, go back to the question. What, for you, are the highlights of this scene?

Act 5, Scene 3

Plot synopsis

Paris and Romeo both come to the monument of the Capulets, Paris to strew Juliet's tomb with flowers, Romeo to join her in death. When Romeo opens the tomb, Paris accosts him, they fight and Paris is killed. Romeo takes poison and dies.

Romeo   O true apothecary,
                  Thy drugs are quick. Thus with a kiss I die.

(lines 119–120)

Friar Lawrence appears just before Juliet wakes. Aware that he is just too late, he attempts at least to bring Juliet away, but soon departs in fear of being discovered himself. Juliet tries to commit suicide by kissing Romeo.

When this fails she stabs herself with Romeo's dagger. Soon the Prince, Montague and the Capulets arrive and Friar Lawrence confesses the truth. All agree that there must be a monument to Romeo and Juliet and that the feud must end.

Text commentary

The Triumph of Love

The Prologue tells us that the 'death-marked love' of the 'star-crossed lovers' will lead to their 'misadventured piteous overthrows'. Here is that tragic ending. However, as the Prologue also tells us, their love will triumph over hatred.

1 Paris dies for love

Romeo   Good gentle youth, tempt not a desperate man;
                  Fly hence and leave me; think upon these gone;
                  Let them affright thee. I beseech thee, youth,
                  Put not another sin upon my head,
                  By urging me to fury. O be gone.

> By heaven, I love thee better than myself,
> For I come hither armed against myself.
> Stay not, be gone, live, and hereafter say,
> A madman's mercy bid thee run away.

(lines 59–67)

You should be very clear why Romeo kills Paris. Paris, knowing only of Romeo's killing of Juliet's cousin, Tybalt, thinks that the 'haughty Montague' plans 'some villainous shame/To the dead bodies' (lines 52–53). He, therefore, provokes the duel. Romeo knows little of the proposed marriage and does not yet recognise Paris, so there is no suggestion of killing his rival in love.

Look at the language of Romeo's speech, which reflects the 'desperate man' he claims to be. Do you think he is threatening Paris or pleading with him? In line 60 he says, 'Fly hence', and in the rest of the speech repeats that idea at least five times. What effect does Shakespeare create with these repetitions? You might like to think back to Act 3, Scene 1, where Romeo also tried to refuse to fight. In both cases the result is the death of a kinsman of the Prince.

It is essential that you read the question very carefully and make sure that you answer all parts of it. Probably there will be a list of suggestions of what you might include in the essay. You do not have to plan your essay around these points, but they are very helpful in pointing you towards useful material.

Paris has not come to the tomb with suicidal intentions like Romeo, but he, too, finds a suitable lover's death.

Paris   O, I am slain. If thou be merciful,
                 Open the tomb, lay me with Juliet.

(lines 72–73)

It is worth thinking about what we have seen of Paris in the play. He has had limited opportunity to show his feelings and audiences assume that his love for Juliet is moderate compared to Romeo's. Here he joins the gathering of lovers united in death. Romeo, the 'madman' who tries to save his life, becomes the 'dead man' who buries him, and you should note the language Romeo uses. Juliet's beauty will illuminate his grave.

 Romeo I'll bury thee in a triumphant grave.

(line 83)

2 Romeo chooses death

Romeo O my love, my wife!
Death, that hath sucked the honey of thy breath,
Hath had no power yet upon thy beauty.
Thou art not conquered; beauty's ensign yet
Is crimson in thy lips and in thy cheeks,
And death's pale flag is not advanced there.

(lines 90–95)

Eyes, look your last.
Arms, take your last embrace. And lips, O you
The doors of breath, seal with a righteous kiss
A dateless bargain to engrossing death.
(*Takes out the poison*) Come, bitter conduct, come
    unsavoury guide,
Thou desperate pilot, now at once run on
The dashing rocks thy sea-sick weary bark.
Here's to my love! (*Drinks*)

(lines 112–119)

 These are extracts from a long final **soliloquy** by Romeo which undergoes many changes of mood, but, despite moments of horror at death, there is never any doubt about the triumph of love.

Let us examine the first extract. It is all based on the **metaphor** of war, Death being the enemy of Love and Beauty. Death has no 'power' and Juliet is not 'conquered'. An 'ensign' is the flag of a regiment and Death's flag has not been able to advance against Beauty. Of course, the **irony** is that Juliet looks alive because she is alive, but, in her actual death and in Romeo's, love is still seen to triumph.

In reading the question take note of key words which instruct you in what to do. If you are asked to compare, you must find similarities and differences between two or more things. If asked to explain, you must show why. Do not automatically tell the story, though you may need to include some narration if you are asked to 'give an account'.

Romeo is sadly weary of the world as he approaches death. The poison is seen as a pilot in a final metaphor of a shipwreck, and Romeo is weary and seasick. Earlier he is also described as weary.

| Romeo | And shake the yoke of inauspicious stars |
| | From this world-wearied flesh. |

(lines 111–112)

Think back to the very start of the play and see if 'inauspicious (unlucky) stars' reminds you of a famous phrase.

However, despite the anguish, you can see Love triumphing in the last embrace and kiss. The phrase 'righteous kiss' means a holy kiss. Romeo and Juliet met with a 'holy palmers' kiss' (1.5, line 97); they part with 'a righteous kiss'. Romeo drinks a last toast to his 'love': Juliet or his feelings or both?

The whole of the scene emphasises Juliet's beauty and also stresses how young the characters are. Romeo calls Paris 'youth' and refers to the youth of dead Tybalt whose body is also in the vault. We feel a great sense of waste, but is it anyone's fault? Romeo says that they are all 'writ ... in sour misfortune's book' (line 82), and later the Friar talks of 'this lamentable chance' (line 146). Is it all bad luck, made up of misunderstandings and unfortunate timing?

3 Juliet wakes to her death

Juliet	Go get thee hence, for I will not away.
	What's here? A cup closed in my true love's hand?
	Poison, I see, hath been his timeless end.
	O churl, drunk all, and left no friendly drop
	To help me after? I will kiss thy lips;
	Haply some poison yet doth hang on them,

	To make me die with a restorative.
	Thy lips are warm.
First Watch	*(within)* Lead, boy. Which way?
Juliet	Yea, noise? Then I'll be brief. O happy dagger!
	(Draws Romeo's dagger)
	This is thy sheath; there rest, and let me die.
	(She stabs herself)

(lines 160–169)

 Juliet's death is an act of love just as Romeo's was. She attempts to die with a kiss, as he did, but actually taking death (poison) from the kiss. Instead she has to die in a powerful union with her lover, as his dagger finds its sheath by stabbing her. You will find words like 'happy' and 'friendly' which might surprise you, but the most unusual choice of word is 'restorative'. Usually this would restore the drinker to life and health. Here it is the poison on Romeo's lips. Juliet sees death and union with Romeo as life, existence without him as less than life.

Friar	A greater power than we can contradict
	Hath thwarted our intents.

(lines 153–155)

What impression do we have of Friar Lawrence in this last scene? He leaves Juliet to die, in his fear of discovery by the watch, though clearly he does not expect her to die. He has (admittedly through bad luck) bungled the whole thing and he insists that it is all the fault of chance or God. His only solution is for Juliet to become a nun.

Look forward to the end of his long narrative explaining events when he says that he is ready to accept punishment if it is seen as his fault.

Friar	let my old life
	Be sacrificed some hour before his time.

(line 266–267)

His execution would come 'some hour' before the natural time of his death: is he so grief-stricken or even guilt-stricken that he cannot bear to live?

Let us consider the various ways in which Love triumphs, though lovers die. We have seen the ways in which Paris', Romeo's and Juliet's deaths affirm the power of love. The last section of the scene shows Love defeating Hate: through the love and deaths of Romeo and Juliet, the feud between the houses ends and Montagues and Capulets affirm love, not enmity.

> **Capulet** As rich shall Romeo by his lady lie,
> Poor sacrifices of our enmity.

(lines 302–303)

Forgiveness is everywhere. Romeo even asks the dead Tybalt for forgiveness in terms that emphasise that Capulet and Montague need not be enemies: 'Forgive me, cousin' (line 101). Nor are the young lovers the only ones driven to the grave by love. What effect has Lady Montague's love for her son had on her (lines 209–210)? Is Lady Capulet's love for her daughter any less (lines 205–206)?

Quiz

Can you trace the plot?

Everything comes together in the Capulets' monument. Can you trace why all the different characters went there?

a) What is Paris' intention in visiting Juliet in the tomb?

b) What prompts Friar Lawrence to go to the tomb? What does he expect to find? What does he think he will need to do?

c) What information has Romeo received that has brought him from Mantua? How is that information inaccurate?

d) Why do the men of the Watch come to investigate?

e) After leaving Juliet, what happens to Friar Lawrence?

f) What rather unlikely reason is given for the arrival of the Prince and the parents?

Can you find the parallels?

Juliet's last speech before taking the drug occurs in Act 4, Scene 3, lines 15–58. Read the following quotations from it and compare them with what happens in the tomb. Look for examples where something similar or something opposite happens.

a) 'What if this mixture do not work at all? ...

No, no, this shall forbid it. Lie thou there.' (Lays down a dagger)

b) 'How if when I am laid into the tomb

I wake before the time that Romeo

Come to redeem me?'

c) 'O look, methinks I see my cousin's ghost

Seeking out Romeo that did spit his body

Upon a rapier's point ...'

d) 'Romeo, I come. This do I drink to thee.'

Do you know these words?

Do you know the meaning of these words, all used in Act 5, Scene 3?

a) 'obsequies' (line 16)

b) 'mattock' (line 22)

c) 'paramour' (line 105)

d) 'sepulchre' (line 141)

e) 'privy' (line 265)

f) 'dateless' (line 115)

g) 'inexorable' (line 38)

h) 'jointure' (line 296)

i) 'inauspicious' (line 111)

j) 'winking' (line 293)

Sample question

From the first few words of the play, we know that Romeo and Juliet will both die at the end. How, then, does Shakespeare maintain a sense of dramatic tension until the last moments of the final scene? You will need to look at:

- *the way he uses dramatic irony,*
- *the way Romeo and Juliet have changed,*
- *the part played by other characters in the scene.*

In your introduction, point out some of the key factors that have led up to this point in the play, including the prologue, mentioned in the title. Point out some of the key quotations from various characters that show there is a sense of inevitability about the ending of the play. We are never allowed to forget that 'these violent delights have violent ends'.

Dramatic irony means that the audience knows something that the characters on stage do not. The deaths in the scene might easily have been prevented if only those involved knew what we know. Paris does not know that Romeo and Juliet are already married and therefore challenges Romeo when he arrives at the tomb. Romeo does not recognise Paris until after he has killed him. Romeo manages to recognise how healthy Juliet looks, but doesn't guess that she is about to wake up. Look at Romeo's speech when he sees Juliet, beginning on line 88, and pick out examples of irony. Explain them.

The number of coincidences also adds to the tension, for example, the fact that Juliet wakes up only after Romeo is dead. What other examples can you find? How do they add to the tension?

Romeo's quiet determination to kill himself is quite different from his frantic attempts to stab himself in Act 3, Scene 3. What effect does this change have on the audience? Look at the difference in language in these two incidents. Find examples and explain them.

How does Shakespeare make Romeo seem older, more in control, more authoritative?

When Juliet awakes to find Romeo dead, how does she react? Compare this with her feelings when she finds out about Tybalt's death? When the friar tries to make Juliet leave, how does their disagreement compare with her argument with her father in Act 3, Scene 5? Why do you think Shakespeare makes her change in this way, moments before her death?

This is essentially Romeo and Juliet's big scene, the inevitable dramatic climax of the play. Even so, other characters are important in developing the sense of tension. Paris choosing just that moment to be in the graveyard, shows that the tragedy has deeply affected others as well. How does his interference at this stage affect our opinion of Romeo? The friar desperately tries to save Juliet. Why does he fail? How do the additional characters, including the families who come in at the end, affect the atmosphere of the scene?

The essay has been concerned with dramatic tension, so in your conclusion it might be worth pointing out that this is released at the very end of the scene. Explain what particularly leads to this feeling of release.

Quiz

ANSWERS

Act 1, Scene 5

Can you trace the plot?

a) Leaves separately, evades them and leaps an orchard wall (presumably the Capulets').

b) The Nurse will come to find Romeo at 9 o'clock to find out what time they are to be married. Romeo, meanwhile, will seek Friar Lawrence's advice.

c) The Friar conducts the service and the Nurse acts as go-between with messages and (later) a rope-ladder. Also very important is that both keep the secret.

d) Romeo, because he is a Montague who dared to gate-crash the Capulets' feast.

e) He is now related to him; two duels occur, not one, both of them fatal.

Can you fill in the background?

a) To introduce a touch of humour, to create the atmosphere of a feast, to give an impression of busy activity, etc.

b) It contrasts both with the youthful love of Romeo and Juliet and the youthful fury of Tybalt. The tone of gentle reminiscence creates a quite different atmosphere from the rest of the scene. It is also one of the scenes where old Capulet appears in a pleasant light.

c) He is hospitable, almost too eager for his guests to enjoy themselves, though he himself is running out of energy. He wishes to make a good impression as head of a great family.

Do you know these words?

a) plate

b) a small supper (not the present meaning of an elaborate meal)
c) faith
d) grotesque or mad-looking (Romeo's mask)
e) marzipan
f) wedding
g) dignified
h) disagree with
i) dance
j) bitterness

ACT 2, SCENES 4 AND 5

Can you trace the character?
a) She praises Paris, though much of her time is spent on reminiscence and sexual humour.
b) In Act 1, Scene 5, she tells each of them who the other is.
c) She will bring Romeo 'to comfort you'.
d) Sound advice as to what to do. All she can advise is to marry Paris because nobody will find out about the other marriage, Romeo being banished.
e) None. Juliet goes on her own to the Friar. The Nurse is as deceived as everyone else.

There are two essential changes. First of all there is the sense of a friendly light-hearted relationship, but this deepens when the Nurse starts to act as go-between. They are close as co-conspirators. When Juliet feels that the Nurse is betraying her morally and emotionally by suggesting she forget about Romeo, the relationship becomes more distant and Juliet acts independently.

Can you finish the sentence?
a) 'Go thy ways, wench, serve God. What, have you dined at home?' (2.5, lines 43–44)
b) 'Doth not rosemary and Romeo begin both with a letter?' (2.4, lines 185–186)
c) 'Where is your mother?' (2.5, line 60)

Do you know these words?
a) swift-winged
b) difficulty
c) tramping
d) fast (flirtatious, flighty) women/girls
e) absolution (we would normally refer to going to confession)

f) perhaps
g) uncontrolled
h) hurry
i) rather
j) universal

ACT 3, SCENE 2

Can you trace the plot?

a) To challenge, insult and fight him, no doubt because of the gate-crashing incident. Romeo reacts mildly because they are now related by marriage.

b) Mercutio feels insulted by his friend's 'vile submission'. His challenge to Tybalt results in his death (Romeo the peacemaker implicated in that) and Romeo's honour drives him to fight and kill Tybalt to avenge his friend.

c) Exile on pain of death. Benvolio makes a sympathetic case for Romeo, but the Prince, who has just lost a kinsman, is determined to stamp out killing.

d) Juliet's love for Tybalt gives her no time or inclination to listen to Paris' advances.

e) He will make the decision for her and the wedding will be on Thursday.

Can you compare the scenes?

a) 1 'Ha, banishment? Be merciful, say 'death' ' (line 12)

2 'For exile hath more terror in his look,
Much more than death.' (lines 13–14)

3 'Hence banished is banished from the world
And world's death is exile.' (lines 19–20)

4 'Calling death 'banished',
Thou cut'st my head off with a golden axe.' (lines 21–22)

5 'And sayest thou yet that exile is not death?' (line 43)

6 'Had'st thou no poison mixed, no sharp-ground knife ...
But 'banished' to kill me?' (lines 44 and 46)

And there are many others!

b) Juliet is alive; Tybalt tried to kill him, but was killed instead; Romeo is banished, not sentenced to death: he can go to Juliet at night; they have future happiness to look forward to when he is pardoned.

c) She repeats the names of Romeo and Tybalt, uses the words 'woeful' (line 85) and 'death' (line 92) and makes many references to weeping.

Do you know these words?

a) know
b) ordinary
c) untrained ('without a man' as well)
d) basilisk, a legendary creature whose look was fatal
e) rear guard
f) deceivers
g) stand to place coffin on
h) chariot-driver
i) ruined
j) brandy or whisky

Act 3, Scene 5

Can you trace the plot?

a) Friar Lawrence: 'I'll to the friar to know his remedy' (line 240). Also she tells the Nurse (line 231) that she is going to his cell 'to make confession', not quite the truth.
b) Provides drug to make her seem dead and plans to inform Romeo.
c) Romeo will come to her when she awakes and take her away to Mantua.
d) Romeo believes her to be really dead, kills Paris and commits suicide. Juliet wakes to find Romeo dead and also commits suicide.
e) Friar John, the messenger to Romeo, is delayed in a plague-infected house and Romeo never receives the message.

Can you identify the image?

a) The coming of night: Phoebus was the Roman sun-god.
b) Night.
c) Juliet's window, 'and Juliet is the sun' rising.
d) Juliet, in Romeo's imagination taking the place of the stars.
e) Romeo 'upon the wings of night'.

Do you know these words?

a) frighten
b) music (also the normal meaning of 'division')
c) water-spout
d) adviser
e) dishcloth
f) doll
g) fugitive (old form of 'renegade')

h) predicting evil
i) estates
j) well connected

Act 5, Scene 3

Can you trace the plot?
a) To strew flowers on her 'bridal bed' and weep over her death.
b) Friar John has just informed him that the message did not reach Romeo. He expects to find Juliet about to wake and plans to reassure her and keep her at his cell.
c) A message from Balthasar that Juliet's 'body sleeps in Capels' monument' (true), and 'her immortal part with angels lives' (false).
d) Paris' page fetches them when Romeo and Paris start fighting.
e) He is found by the Watch leaving the churchyard with his digging implements.
f) People in the street are crying the names of Romeo, Juliet and Paris and running towards the monument: how did the news break so quickly?

Can you find the parallels?
a) The mixture works, but the plan goes wrong and a dagger becomes the last resort when there is no poison left.
b) The opposite of what happens – a sad irony.
c) Romeo sees his death as being a 'favour' to the dead Tybalt.
d) Romeo drinks to 'my love' before taking poison and kissing Juliet; she tries to die by taking the poison from his lips.

Do you know these words?
a) ceremonies for the dead
b) pick-axe
c) lover
d) tomb
e) in the know, aware of the secret
f) eternal
g) unyielding
h) estate given by groom to bride in marriage
i) unfortunate
j) turning a blind eye, neglecting